P9-CDZ-039

WILLIMANTIC PUBLIC LIBRARY

3 4036 11398 4680

j
646.77
HEI

10-1214

$32.79

**Willimantic Public Library**
**Children's Department**
905 Main St.
Willimantic, CT. 06226
(860) 465-3082

DEMCO

# I Luv U 2

## Understanding Relationships and Dating

ABDO
Publishing Company

# A GUY'S GUIDE

# I Luv U 2

## Understanding Relationships and Dating

by Pete Heiden

**Content Consultant**
**Dr. Robyn J. A. Silverman**
**Child/Teen Development Expert and Success Coach**
**Powerful Words Character Development**

# Credits

Published by ABDO Publishing Company, 8000 West 78th Street, Edina, Minnesota 55439. Copyright © 2011 by Abdo Consulting Group, Inc. International copyrights reserved in all countries. No part of this book may be reproduced in any form without written permission from the publisher. The Essential Library™ is a trademark and logo of ABDO Publishing Company.

Printed in the United States of America,
North Mankato, Minnesota
062010
092010

THIS BOOK CONTAINS AT LEAST 10% RECYCLED MATERIALS.

Editor: Melissa Johnson
Copy Editor: Nick Cafarelli
Interior Design and Production: Marie Tupy
Cover Design: Craig Hinton

**Library of Congress Cataloging-in-Publication Data**
Heiden, Pete.
 I luv U 2 : understanding relationships and dating / Pete Heiden ; content consultant, Robyn J.A. Silverman.
     p. cm. — (Essential health : a guy's guide)
  ISBN 978-1-61613-541-6
 1.  Man-woman relationships. 2.  Dating (Social customs)  I. Silverman, Robyn J. A. II. Title. III. Title: I love you too.
  HQ801.H4287 2011
  305.3—dc22
                                        2010017058

**WILLIMANTIC PUBLIC LIBRARY**
**CHILDREN'S DEPARTMENT**
    10-1214

# contents

Meet Dr. Robyn . . . . . . . . . . . . . . . . . . . . . . . . . . . . . . . . . . . 6

Take It from Me . . . . . . . . . . . . . . . . . . . . . . . . . . . . . . . . . . . 8

Chapter 1. Make-out Mistake . . . . . . . . . . . . . . . . . . 10

Chapter 2. Big Questions . . . . . . . . . . . . . . . . . . . . . 20

Chapter 3. The Next Step . . . . . . . . . . . . . . . . . . . . . 28

Chapter 4. Tongue-tied . . . . . . . . . . . . . . . . . . . . . . . 36

Chapter 5. Not Quite Ready . . . . . . . . . . . . . . . . . . 46

Chapter 6. Insecurity . . . . . . . . . . . . . . . . . . . . . . . . . 56

Chapter 7. Feeling Forgotten . . . . . . . . . . . . . . . . . 66

Chapter 8. Moral Dilemma . . . . . . . . . . . . . . . . . . . 76

Chapter 9. Breaking Up . . . . . . . . . . . . . . . . . . . . . . 84

Chapter 10. Rumor Has It. . . . . . . . . . . . . . . . . . . . . 94

A Second Look . . . . . . . . . . . . . . . . . . . . . . . . . . . . . . . 102

Pay It Forward . . . . . . . . . . . . . . . . . . . . . . . . . . . . . . . 104

Additional Resources . . . . . . . . . . . . . . . . . . . . . . . . 106

Glossary. . . . . . . . . . . . . . . . . . . . . . . . . . . . . . . . . . . . . . 108

Index . . . . . . . . . . . . . . . . . . . . . . . . . . . . . . . . . . . . . . . . 110

About the Author. . . . . . . . . . . . . . . . . . . . . . . . . . . . 112

Dr. Robyn Silverman truly enjoys spending time with young people. In fact, it's what she does best! As a child and teen development specialist, Dr. Robyn has devoted her career to helping guys just like you become all they can be—and possibly more than they ever imagined. Throughout this series, you'll read her expert advice on friends, girls, classmates, school, family, and everything in between.

A self-esteem and body image expert, Dr. Robyn takes a positive approach to life. She knows how tough it is to be a kid in today's world, and she's prepared with encouragement and guidance to help you become your very best and realize your goals.

Dr. Robyn helps young people share their wildest dreams and biggest problems. Her compassion, openness, and honesty make her trusted by many adolescents, and she considers it a gift to be able to interact with the young people whom she sees as the leaders of tomorrow. She created the Powerful Words Character Development system, a program taught all over the world in martial arts and other sports programs to help guys just like you become examples to others in their communities.

As a speaker, success coach, and award-winning author, Dr. Robyn's powerful messages have reached thousands of people. Her expert advice has been featured in *Prevention* magazine, *Parenting* magazine, *U.S. News and World Report*, and the *Washington Post*. She was an expert for *The Tyra Show*, *Fox News,* and NBC's *LXtv.* She has an online presence, too. You can follow her on Twitter, become a fan on Facebook, and read her blog on her Web site, www.DrRobynSilverman.com. When she isn't working, Dr. Robyn enjoys spending time with her family in New Jersey.

Dr. Robyn believes that young people are assets to be developed, not problems to be fixed. As she puts it, "Guys are so much more than the way the media paints them. They have so many things to offer. I'm ready to highlight how guys get it right and tips for the ways they can make their teen years the best years so far . . . I'd be grateful if you'd come along for the ride."

# Take It from Me

Many children spend most of their time with their parents, siblings, and perhaps a few neighbors or close friends. When a guy gets older, he usually begins to form friendships with a wider group of people. Relationships are a big aspect of our adolescent years, forcing us to adjust to shifting conditions. Our relationships might seem to be in constant turmoil, changing as we redefine who we are and who our friends are.

During the earliest phase of my adolescence, one of my best friends was a girl named Sarah. For almost two years, she and I were inseparable. But then I moved away to a big city in another state where I had to adjust to a completely new set of friends and conditions. It was hard being the outsider. The new kids seemed so sophisticated to me. Many of my new friends were dating, but I wasn't. I didn't meet any guys who had a close friendship with a girl like the one I once had. In fact, they laughed when I told them about her and thought I was making it up. I became shy and didn't talk much to girls for a long time after that. Then we moved to yet another state and I had to start over again establishing a new group of friends.

As I got a little older, I found it got a bit easier to talk to girls. I became close friends with some girls and dated others. At times, it was confusing to determine who should be in which category. Looking back now on that early friendship, I can see how Sarah taught me much more about relating to girls than I could have guessed at the time. I think that relationship has benefited and influenced me throughout my life. And yes, all these years later, I still miss her.

I hope the relationships you experience over the next few years are as fun and rewarding for you as mine have been for me. This book shares the stories of other guys like you as they face challenges and pitfalls in their relationships as adolescents. I hope these stories help you face and overcome your own challenges in the coming years.

Best of luck,
Pete

# 1

# Make-out Mistake

**N**o one likes to make a mistake. Fumbling the throw to third base to lose the game can be embarrassing. Yet some mistakes are worse than losing a game. The more serious the mistake, the worse it feels. You might become frightened and confused about what to do. You might even convince yourself that you can't make it right again, even though it is rare that a mistake cannot be corrected.

When making a mistake that involves a friend, how you deal with that mistake can either destroy a friendship or strengthen it. A guy's first instinct might be to avoid the person or people he harmed—even if the whole thing was completely unintentional. However, as with all relationship issues, communicating with the other person is very important. Communication can help you correct the error and mend the friendship.

Malcolm was influenced by what he thought everyone else was doing and made a big mistake. Read his story to see how he eventually tried to correct it.

## Malcolm's Story

Malcolm had gone with a big group of friends to the lake. They spent the afternoon swimming and playing volleyball. Late in the afternoon, they

*when making a mistake that involves a friend, how you deal with that mistake can either destroy a friendship or strengthen it.*

grilled hot dogs and burgers. As they finished eating, they started to break up into smaller groups. Couples began drifting away, and soon only Malcolm and a few other kids were left sitting around the tables. Among them was Malcolm's friend Karen. He had met her in Spanish class the year before. Malcolm moved over to Karen's table.

"What's up?" he asked.

"Not much," she replied. As they chatted about school, they realized they were the only two people left sitting at the picnic tables.

"Huh . . . everyone's gone," remarked Malcolm.

"Let's go for a walk, too," suggested Karen.

As Malcolm and Karen walked, they saw pairs of kids here and there sitting together under trees and on the beach. It seemed to Malcolm they were all making out.

"Really subtle, you guys," he said as they passed one couple. "Looks like the fishing was good," he said, laughing, as they passed another.

Malcolm got quiet as he realized everyone was paired up and making out. That is, everyone but him.

## Think About It

- why do you think Malcolm felt as though everyone else was forming couples and kissing?

- why do you think Malcolm was teasing the couples as he walked past them in the park?

Walking along the shore, Karen spotted a nice log to sit on.

"Hey look, our own secluded spot," she said. "We can watch the sun go down."

The log was perfectly angled to catch the lowering sun, and bushes screened it from everyone they could see. They sat down and soaked up the warmth and watched as the guys fishing across the lake moved along the shore until they were out of sight around the point.

Malcolm leaned over and kissed Karen. She was startled but didn't get up and leave. Malcolm was encouraged, so he kissed her again. Soon they were making out like the other couples, and for a moment Malcolm didn't feel left out. Suddenly though, Malcolm found himself wondering why he was making out with a friend.

*Malcolm got quiet as he realized everyone was paired up and making out. That is, everyone but him.*

They were friends, but he had never been attracted to her as a girlfriend. Now, sitting here making out with her, he felt funny. He felt kissing Karen was okay, but he also felt awkward, like he was doing something stupid. He sensed Karen was disinterested, and he wondered if she felt as funny doing this as he now did.

They stopped making out and sat without speaking. Malcolm realized he had made a big mistake, and he wondered what he should do or say. Feeling like a fool, he didn't say anything. After a little while they got up and walked back to the picnic area. Embarrassed now, Karen and Malcolm joined different groups as everyone headed home.

## Think About It

- Have you ever felt pressure to kiss someone or kissed someone because you wanted to know what it feels like?

- Have you ever kissed someone and felt "funny" or embarrassed afterward?

- Why do you suppose Malcolm feels he has made a big mistake?

- What actions do you think Malcolm could have taken when he felt that he should "do or say" something?

A few days later, Malcolm saw Karen again when a group of his friends got together to hang out at the mall. He felt embarrassed to be near her and wondered what he could possibly say to her. As the group walked around, he and Karen stayed away from each other. When the group stopped by the food court, Malcolm was focused on ordering. He was startled to find himself standing next to Karen.

"Hey Karen," he said looking directly at her for the first time all day.

"Hi," she replied, quickly looking away.

"Karen?"

"What do you want?"

"Um, I just . . . I'm sorry. You know, about the lake stuff."

Getting their food, Karen and Malcolm found a table and sat together.

"I don't know why it happened but . . . I thought everyone . . . no, I didn't think . . . I . . . well, I'm sorry."

"I've been wondering why I let you," Karen admitted. "I should have stopped, but . . ."

"I still don't know what I was thinking," Malcolm interrupted. "It just seemed that everyone was together but us."

"We *were* together. We were walking and . . . "

"No, I mean making out. I just felt . . . I don't know . . . like the only one who wasn't really with someone . . ." continued Malcolm.

"I know that feeling," said Karen.

"It was dumb," admitted Malcolm.

"You think it's dumb kissing me?" asked Karen. "Thanks!"

"No! Yes! You know what I mean. It was dumb of me to do that when you're my friend, not my girlfriend," he stammered. "At least, I hope you're still my friend."

"I . . ."

"Hey, Karen," called Karen's friend Teresa as she ran up to the table and interrupted them. "Come on, the movie is starting." Teresa grabbed Karen's hand and pulled her up and away toward the theaters.

"Wait," Karen exclaimed turning back toward Malcolm. "Thanks for apologizing!" Then smiling like her old self, she asked him, "Are you coming with us?"

## Think About It

- why do you think Karen looked away from Malcolm when he spoke to her at the mall?

- why do you think Malcolm looked directly at Karen when he spoke to her?

- Do you think that Karen and Malcolm could have continued being good friends if they didn't speak to one another about the kiss?

Experimenting with kissing or making out is a natural part of growing up. It is when we give in to peer pressure or go further than we are prepared to that we become uncomfortable. Malcolm's and Karen's curiosity in itself didn't create their embarrassment. The problem was that they kissed because everyone else was doing it.

When you become embarrassed for making a mistake in a social setting, you may want to run away and hide, but this will not fix the problem. If you make a mistake in front of a friend, try talking to him or her about it. A sincere apology can help mend many problems.

Respect is very important. If you or your partner is uncomfortable with kissing or any other form of touching, you need to stop immediately.

## Work It Out

1.  When you feel that you have made a mistake, decide what the healthiest action might have been. Then, try to take this new action next time.

2. Eliminate confusion by verbally asking permission to kiss. Kissing a friend is a very intimate experience. Consider it your job to do this because your friend might be too nervous to speak up.

3. Ask questions and talk about what you are feeling. This can be very scary and difficult at first, but it will ease your mind and reassure your friend that you care.

4. When speaking to someone who has been avoiding you, make direct eye contact with that person and say you would like to talk. Eye contact will help you both feel more confident.

## The Last Word from Pete

Many times an unspoken apology is all that stands between a guy and a lost friendship. When you find you are unable to speak to another person about a problem, you may have a friend who can act as a middleman and help you start the conversation. Remember, you are learning new social skills—and communicating is an important one. If you learn to overcome your fear and embarrassment, you will find it easier to speak to others when you do need to correct a mistake.

# Big Questions

 dolescence is filled with big questions. Who should I hang with? Who should I date? What is acceptable to our families, our friends, or to us? One big question for many adolescents is their sexual identity. Am I heterosexual? Am I homosexual? Who am I attracted to, or what type of relationship do I need to feel understood? With whom can I be my true self? These are not easy questions to answer, even for adults. We might be surprised by the answers we find.

We might search for our answers by physically trying things out, by talking to our friends, or by exploring the questions through our imaginations. Sometimes when we examine a question deeply, however, we just find more questions.

## Ned's Story

Ned and Luis had several classes together. In class, they discovered that they

Sometimes when we examine a question deeply, however, we just find more questions.

had a lot in common. Halfway through first semester, they decided to get together at Luis's house to study and work on a team project for English.

Ned and Luis played computer games in Luis's room for a while before pulling out their books. They settled in, discussed the project, and started reading. Before long, a plot twist in their assigned novel reminded Ned of a new rumor he'd heard in school that day.

"Did you hear that Spencer and Maria broke up?" Ned remarked, looking up from his book.

"Really?" asked Luis. "What happened?"

"Rachel told me that Maria said that Spencer tried to get her to go all the way. That's why she dumped him."

"Too bad for Spencer," said Luis. "Can't blame him for trying, though."

"You really think that?" asked Ned. "I think Spencer shouldn't have tried to push Maria."

"I might have tried, too, if I were Spencer."

"Really? You're saying you're ready to have sex?" Ned challenged.

"Yeah," said Luis. "Well, okay, I don't know. But who's going to admit they're not ready? The guys would say I was weird, or gay."

"Well I . . ." began Ned. Luis's mother knocked on the door, interrupting Ned.

## Think About It

- Do you know someone who has felt pressured to have sex? How did it make that person feel?

- Do your friends or classmates tease people if they admit they are not ready to have sex?

- Have you ever thought about how old a person should be to have sex? How old do you think that is?

"I've got cookies for you guys," she said. "Are you working hard?"

"Yeah, Mom," replied Luis. "Thanks!"

The guys went back to work, grabbing an occasional cookie. At one point, their hands brushed as they both went for the same cookie. Ned felt hot for a second, like his face was flushed, but Luis didn't seem to notice anything. Ned buried his nose in his book and kept quiet.

Ned's thoughts kept wandering back to their interrupted conversation.

"Hey," he asked, "have you ever wondered what it would be like to do it?"

"Sometimes," Luis replied. "But I've seen some of my older brother's movies, and everyone seems to like it a lot."

"I dunno," said Ned. "It looks totally weird. And I can't imagine taking my clothes off in front of a girl. What if she laughs at me?"

"If she really likes you she won't laugh," Luis reassured him.

The boys went back to their books again, but Ned couldn't concentrate on what he was reading. A few minutes passed, and he looked up again.

"Why do you think people do it, anyway?" asked Ned, giving up on his book.

"I'm not sure, maybe because they like each other?" replied Luis, leaning forward.

It was quiet for a few moments. Then Ned added, "It should be more than that. Not just because someone is hot, either. I want someone who gets me, you know?"

Luis nodded but didn't say anything. Ned filled the uncomfortable silence with news of the latest YouTube video he had watched. Luis, still thinking about Ned's question, didn't hear him. Interrupting Ned, he smiled as he said, "I think I want those things, too."

"Fame on YouTube?" laughed Ned.

"The trust thing. I think it's important, too, like, when you're with a girl—you know, really *with* her."

"Oh yeah," smiled Ned, "right."

"Why can't we talk to girls this way?" asked Luis. "It seems so much easier talking to a guy."

Ned laughed and said, "Yeah, girls seem totally messed up. With a guy you don't have to play games. You don't have to be so careful with what you say."

As Ned talked, he watched Luis brush the hair back off his face. He realized he was staring when Luis exclaimed, "Dude, you checking me out?"

"No, I'm not," exclaimed Ned, looking away.

"Then quit staring at me like that," said Luis.

A long awkward silence followed as Ned thought to himself, *I like being with Luis. We understand each other. Am I checking him out?*

## Think About It

- Do you have friends or family members with whom you feel you can talk honestly about dating, kissing, or having sexual intercourse?

- Do you think it's easier to talk to other guys than girls? Why or why not?

- Have you ever looked at someone for a moment longer than what felt appropriate? What were you thinking or feeling? What happened next?

As we develop sexually, we become aware of differences in ourselves and others. It is not uncommon to find yourself staring. You might be staring because you are physically attracted, or you might be noticing a developmental change you haven't seen before. Maybe you just zoned out!

If this happens to you, you might begin to question your own sexuality. Both homosexual and heterosexual boys can experience this. It means that your emotional and physical self are developing rapidly, and you have a lot of changes to process. Changes often mean questions!

You may feel confused or even anxious by what you are feeling or thinking. This is normal for everyone. As you talk with your peers about what you all are experiencing, you may find some answers. But if the anxiety and confusion become overwhelming, you should seek out a trusted and knowledgeable adult with whom you can discuss your concerns.

## Work It Out

1. Talk about it. Just as you have many questions about sex, sexuality, and dating, so do your friends.

2. If you're having questions about your sexuality, talk to your parents or another trusted adult. An adult can help you find reputable information to help you work through your confusion.

3. If you feel uncomfortable talking to people, check some books out at the library or browse reputable Web sites, such as the ones listed in this book.

## The Last Word from Pete

Many times we are confused by our feelings or attractions. You may worry if your feelings are normal, or if you yourself are normal. These are common questions that everyone has in some form or other. Whatever sexual identity feels right to you, remember that you are normal and that there are millions of other guys like you.

If, however, you find you have serious concerns over your sexual identity, you may have a counselor at school you can talk to. If your school doesn't have a counselor, or you are reluctant to take advantage of this service, there are organizations with Web sites that you can look for to help answer many of your questions.

# 3
# The Next Step

In many ways, adolescence is defined by change. Change is especially common in friendships. You might lose some friends gradually as your interests change. You might have a disagreement so strong that it causes a falling out. You might find yourself revising your definition of "best friend." You will make new friends, too.

Once in a while, a romance may even blossom between close friends. Knowing a friendship has just dramatically changed doesn't necessarily mean that it has ended. But if it hasn't ended, how do you redefine it? If nothing else, the adolescent years are filled with surprises.

One summer, Jason's feelings for his best friend began to shift. He doesn't know exactly what happened, but he knows that nothing is quite the same anymore.

## Jason's Story

Jason and Amy were best friends. Jason admired Amy's independence. He didn't know anyone else who could climb a tree or ride a bike as fast and as far as she could. Jason could talk to Amy about books instead of just the latest sitcom. He believed he could talk to her about anything.

*One summer, Jason's feelings for his best friend began to shift. He knows that nothing is quite the same anymore.*

One afternoon, Jason decided to walk to the comic store to see if they had any new Japanese anime. On his way there, he saw Amy sitting in the park. He went over to say hi and noticed Amy was crying. "Hey Jason," Amy called, "I'm so glad to see you. I need a friend right now."

Jason sat down on the bench next to her. "What's wrong?" he asked. Amy told him that this day was the anniversary of her father's death.

"Aw, I'm sorry," said Jason, not knowing what else to say. Fortunately Amy jumped in, reminiscing about her dad.

"He taught me to not be afraid to climb trees," Amy began, "and how to ride a bike." Amy paused, remembering, and a tear rolled down her cheek. "My dad was always there, cheering me on. I wish I could tell you how much I miss him, but . . . but . . . "

Amy choked on her words and then threw her head on Jason's shoulder, sobbing. Although he and Amy had held hands in the past, and always gave a hug to say hello or good-bye, this moment felt different to Jason. He felt awkward and sat stiffly for a moment before slowly putting his arm around her.

## Think About It

- Amy says she needs a friend. What do you think she means?

- Do you have any friends who are girls?

- Do you think that having a friendship with a girl is different from having a friendship with a guy? Why or why not?

As Jason and Amy sat embracing one another in silence, Jason struggled with his thoughts and feelings, which were tangled and confused. On the one hand, he felt sympathy for Amy and her loss. He wanted to say something—but what? Jason had never lost anyone close to him. He wanted to tell her it would be all right, but that sounded dumb to him. Even saying "I'm sorry" seemed childish.

On the other hand, Jason felt something strange and new. It felt good to have Amy close against him, making physical contact. This made him feel important and needed by her. He thought he'd like to tell her so, but the timing didn't seem right. He wondered if he was selfish for feeling something like this while

*Although he and Amy had held hands in the past, and always gave a hug to say hello or good-bye, this moment felt different to Jason.*

his friend was so distraught. Jason wished he could just talk to Amy about what he was experiencing, but he remained silent.

After a while, Amy sat up, drying her eyes. "I should get going," she whispered to Jason.

"Okay," he nodded. "Can I walk you home, though?"

Amy agreed, "Yeah, that sounds nice."

As Jason and Amy drew close to her house, Amy thanked Jason for listening and apologized to him for crying.

Jason shrugged his shoulders. "That's okay. I don't mind."

Amy smiled. "Just you being here makes me feel better."

She gave him a quick hug. It startled him a little, but he didn't say anything. He still didn't know what he could say.

"Bye, Jason," continued Amy. She looked a lot happier as she went into her house. "See ya tomorrow!"

Jason headed home feeling very confused about everything that had happened. He felt stupid for not being able to think of anything to say after his friend shared so much. He remembered Amy saying she liked it that he just listened to her. *She even thanked me for it*, he told himself. Still, he didn't feel he had been very helpful.

Jason wondered why his best friend's sadness could make him feel so good inside. He found himself thinking he would like to have her head on his shoulder again. He found himself wanting to hold her close. Jason wanted so much to talk to his best friend about what he was feeling, but as he reached his house Jason felt that his friendship with Amy had somehow changed. Standing outside his door, Jason realized he was afraid and wondered how he could talk to Amy tomorrow about how he now felt.

## Think About It

- Have you ever consoled someone and felt that your words were inadequate?

- why do you think Amy felt better even though Jason said very little?

- what do you think changed in Jason's friendship with Amy?

Friendships have many things in common with romantic relationships. Both involve close companionship, and the social skills used to communicate between the parties are often the same. Holding a friend close to comfort her creates an intimately physical and highly emotional experience for the guy. It's a normal reaction for a guy to find himself looking at her with new eyes.

In talking to the girl about how you now feel after the experience, you could begin by describing the event and then talking about how the experience has affected you. As you describe your feelings, try to use neutral words or phrases. You could explain how good it felt to put your arm around her or tell her how happy talking to her makes you feel. These types of actions might help her to see you in a new light, too.

## Work It Out

1. Being a good friend does not mean that you have all of the answers. Some problems are too big for anyone to solve, such as the death of a loved one. Sometimes, just listening is the right thing to do.

2. When experiencing a mix of emotions, ask yourself questions: Why do I feel confused about this? What do I really want to do about this? What should I do to make it happen?

3. If you find yourself experiencing new, deeper feelings for a friend, it's okay to share them. Then, listen to what your friend says in return. If you communicate, together you can figure out if your relationship should change.

4. Say "thank you" to your friends when they have been helpful. A little appreciation goes a long way in building relationships.

## The Last Word from Pete

It is not unusual to develop a physical attraction to a best friend. Go ahead and talk to her, but don't try to rush things. She may tell you she would really enjoy dating you, or she might not feel the same way. Remember, just because she is your friend does not mean she feels the same romantic attraction. Listen to what she has to say, as you always have. Besides, even if your friend isn't interested at first, if you are patient and supportive, there is a chance that she may change her mind down the road.

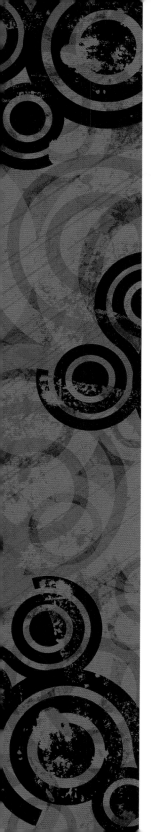

# 4

# Tongue-tied

Some guys find it difficult to speak with a girl they really like. Fear of making a mistake or saying something embarrassing might keep you quiet. Then again, you may be afraid of rejection or nervous about what you should say. This is easy to understand—no one wants to look foolish.

You may think it's only the shy boys who get tongue-tied, but sometimes, even boys who normally speak easily with girls can find themselves at a loss for words. Often it is our unspoken fears that end up making us do the most foolish things. Even when we know our fears are foolish, we allow those fears to

keep us from succeeding. Sometimes we need a little help to get through the situation.

## Mario's Story

Mario thought Jessica was the most beautiful girl in school. Her father had just transferred to the nearby army base, so she had entered Mario's school in October. She quickly became popular and hung out with some of the people in Mario's circle of friends. All winter, Mario wanted to speak with Jessica. He had no problem talking to the girls he'd known since elementary school, but he

You may think it's only the shy boys who get tongue-tied, but sometimes, even boys who normally speak easily with girls can find themselves at a loss for words.

was always tongue-tied when he got near her. With the big spring dance rapidly approaching, Mario wanted to take Jessica more than anything.

## Think About It

- why do you think Mario finds it so difficult to talk to Jessica?

- Have you ever been tongue-tied or shy around someone? If so, why do you think this happened?

- what could Mario do to make talking to Jessica easier?

Mario gelled his hair, doused himself in body spray, and picked his coolest outfits every day for a week as he worked up the courage to ask Jessica out.

Finally, Mario decided he would ask her on Thursday morning before classes. He went to school early and waited for her near her locker. When he saw her coming down the hall, however, he panicked and ran off to talk to a group of his friends.

"Hey, there she is," urged his best friend Casey. "Now is your chance."

"How can I ask her?" moaned Mario. "I've never said a thing to her."

Casey reassured him Jessica was nice. "Just ask her out," he told Mario. "She won't laugh at you."

Friday after school as Mario was heading home, he bumped into Jessica on the school steps. Jessica said, "Hi!" and smiled at him.

Mario looked down at his hands as he struggled with his words. Finally, he mumbled, "Hi."

For a moment things were quiet. Then Jessica said, "I have to get going."

"Yeah," muttered Mario. As Jessica turned to walk away, Mario coughed to clear his throat and finally looked up at her.

*when he saw her coming down the hall, however, he panicked and ran off to talk to a group of his friends.*

"Jessica, are you going to the dance?"

Jessica turned back to him and smiled before answering. "No one asked me," she said.

"Would you go with me?" Mario asked.

"That'd be cool," she beamed.

## Think About It

- Have you ever tried to invite someone to a dance or an event? What happened? How did it make you feel?

- Could Casey have helped Mario in any other ways? What would you do if you were Casey in this situation?

All the way home, Mario felt ecstatic. He had done it! True, he had stumbled into asking her, but he had asked her! And Jessica had not laughed at him. She would actually go with him!

Over the weekend, however, Mario's excitement quickly turned back into nervousness. He spent the next couple of days thinking about all the things he didn't know about taking a girl out. In his head, Mario began to consider everything that could go wrong. What could he talk to her about? He had only spoken to her that one time and that seemed like ages ago.

> Mario's excitement quickly turned back into nervousness. He spent the next couple of days thinking about all the things he didn't know about taking a girl out.

He had a vague notion that people went out to eat before dances. He had no idea what Jessica might like to eat. Where could he take her to eat? And would his mom have to drive them everywhere? How would he afford it? What if he spilled something on her dress? He would look clumsy. In the movies, he'd seen guys bring their dates flowers, too. What if she didn't like flowers, or worse, what if she was allergic to them and had to go to the hospital? Everyone would laugh at him then. Mario hadn't even considered that he would have to dance. *Oh my God*, he remembered, *I don't know how to dance.*

## Think About It

- Have you ever felt nervous about what you might be expected to do during a date?

- What advice would you give Mario to help him feel less nervous?

By Saturday night, Mario's nerves were beginning to get the best of him. In the bathroom that night, he washed his face and then just stood there, staring at himself in the mirror.

*What does she see in me?* he thought. *Why did I ask her out?*

When Mario had been in there a while, Mario's dad came and knocked on the door.

"Are you okay in there?" his dad called. "Are you sick?"

Mario opened the door slowly and walked out.

"You don't look so good," remarked his dad. "What's wrong?"

"Nothing," shrugged Mario.

"Doesn't look like nothing," pressed his dad.

"Well, so, okay, there's this girl . . ." Mario's fears about the date poured out in a rush.

"Whoa!" said his dad. "Calm down. Let's take this step by step."

"Okay," said Mario, taking a few deep breaths.

"First, dancing. You don't need to know any steps or anything. Move back and forth to the music. Just enjoy yourself, and it should come naturally. The men in our family have natural rhythm," his dad added, winking.

"What about dinner and flowers and stuff?" asked Mario.

"Why don't you ask some of your other friends who are going to the dance to go out to dinner as a group? Being in a group might make conversation easier. You'll be less nervous with your friends there, too. Your mom and I will give you some money for dinner and flowers. And I'm sure Mom would love to help you pick a shirt and tie to wear."

"Thanks, Dad," said Mario, breathing a sigh of relief. Things didn't sound so complicated, after all. And going to dinner with a group of friends would be fun!

## Think About It

- Have you ever been on a date? What did you do? How did it go? Would you do anything differently in the future?

- Did Mario's dad give him good advice? Would you tell Mario to do anything differently?

Being afraid to speak to someone you like can be a difficult and stressful situation. If it's someone you know only from a distance, it can make the situation even more anxiety provoking. Mario managed to clear the biggest hurdle—getting Jessica to say yes—but then started to panic when he considered the possible outcomes of their date. Luckily, Mario's dad was there to offer advice.

Most of Mario's fears centered on doing something wrong or embarrassing himself. These fears were caused mostly by a lack of experience. Knowing how to ask someone out and knowing what to do on a date are skills like any other. With practice and experience, Cody will become more sure of himself.

It's often less difficult to speak to a girl when you are both hanging out with a larger group of friends. This is one benefit of participating in group activities with your circle of friends; in a group, there's less pressure talking to a girl than during a one-on-one date.

## Work It Out

1.  If you are nervous, talking to friends, parents, or other support people can help. Tell them what you would like to happen,

and why you are nervous. By doing this, you are also preparing them to catch you if you fall.

2. Give yourself a break. Asking someone to date you for the first time can be scary because you've never done it before. It may take a little practice, you might make a few mistakes, and, yes, you may receive a few rejections. In many cases, the other person is likely as nervous as you are.

3. Be yourself. You don't need to wear special clothing, talk differently, or spend money in order to ask someone out on a date.

## The Last Word from Pete

There is no reason to stress yourself over asking a girl out or going on a date. Try to keep a sense of humor—most girls won't bite! Relax! It might be hard to believe, but your date and everyone else around you are just as worried about doing something embarrassing as you are. Remember that your friends have been experiencing the same fears, and they may be helpful in getting you over the scary parts. Your parents or other trusted adults have probably experienced many similar situations and may have useful tips to share. Be yourself, have fun, and things most likely will turn out all right.

# 5

# Not Quite Ready

In today's society, it is generally accepted that adolescents will begin dating. And yet, not everyone is ready to date at the same age. This isn't surprising; we all develop at different rates. Knowing that should make it easy to see that it's normal for some guys not to be ready or interested in dating as soon as some of their friends and classmates.

Sometimes, you just want to be left alone to do your own thing. But what if doing your own thing is different from what your peers are doing? You might feel left out or worry that you aren't normal. It can be difficult to get support from your peers if they perceive you as different. If most of his classmates are dating, a guy who doesn't date might be questioned or taunted by the other guys. Even good-natured teasing from friends can hurt.

## Satish's Story

As Satish walked down the school hall, Emily and Ashley cooed, "Hi, Satish."

Marie came up to walk beside him. She asked, "Hey Satish, can you still help me with my lines tonight?"

"Sure, Marie," he replied. "After basketball practice. I'll meet you outside the gym."

The girls all liked Satish. They knew he didn't date, and they all wondered why. Leaving flowery notes in his locker was their friendly way of teasing him. The girls clustered around Satish as he reached his locker and opened it. The scent of perfume wafted past him and swirled down the hall. The girls giggled as he discovered their surprise.

*Sometimes, you just want to be left alone to do your own thing. But what if doing your own thing is different from what your peers are doing?*

*Just what I need today,* thought Satish. He picked up the note that fell onto the floor and quickly stuffed it into his gym bag. "Why did they have to put perfume on it?" he said to himself, knowing the other guys were going to give him a hard time now. Ever since that big-mouth Alfonso found out about the notes, life had been hard on him. Satish wasn't the only guy not dating, but for some reason he had become the target. Lately it was getting worse. *Nothing like having a big bull's-eye on my back,* he thought.

"Hi, Satish," Alfonso snickered, coming up behind him. "Get your perfume in the girl aisle?"

"Get lost," replied Satish, slamming his locker and heading for class.

"You're supposed to give that to girls, not wear it yourself, stupid," Alfonso taunted.

"Leave him alone," said Ann as she passed Alfonso.

Alfonso just laughed as he walked off to class in the other direction.

## Think About It

- why do you think the girls tease Satish with flowery notes and perfume?

- why do you think girls like Satish?

- why do you think the guys pick on Satish about not being ready to date?

By the end of the day, a group of guys was claiming Satish wore perfume. In the locker room getting ready for practice, a few guys snickered at him. Satish could hear them making cracks about other feminine products he might use. *Why can't they leave me alone?* thought Satish as he slowly walked out to the gym.

"Vanilla?" sniffed Coach Ramirez, smiling as Satish walked by him onto the court. "One of my favorites."

As Satish flinched, Coach Ramirez's smile dropped. "The guys giving you grief over those notes?"

Satish stopped and looked at his coach with surprise. "How'd you know about the notes?" he asked.

"Come on over to the bleachers so we can talk," his coach said. "Gerry," he called over his shoulder to his assistant, "run 'em through dribbling drills and practice shooting off the dribble."

Turning back to Satish, he continued, "Everyone knows. Some of the guys are getting jealous."

"They aren't jealous. Trust me."

"They're jealous because they think all the girls like you."

"Yeah, they like to give me crap."

"They wouldn't tease you if they didn't like you. The girls feel safe with you, Satish, because you don't pressure them like some of the other boys do."

"What do you mean?"

"You pay attention to them, but you aren't trying to impress them or make out with them. The girls don't have to be on guard with you, so they can relax and enjoy the time they spend with you."

"Yeah, but the other guys date."

"So what?" asked Mr. Ramirez. "Don't rush into something just because you 'think' everyone else is doing it. That's not a real reason to do anything. If you're not ready to date yet, it's no big deal."

"It feels like a big deal," Satish said, looking down at his shoes.

## Think About It

- In what ways do girls let you and your friends know that they appreciate your friendship?

- How important is dating to you right now in your life?

- What reasons do you think a person might have for not being ready to date?

- Do you or your friends feel that maybe you should be dating even if you aren't ready?

"You have me there," laughed Mr. Ramirez, "I remember when I was your age and it seemed like a big deal to me too."

"I'd like to ask someone out . . . but . . . I'm, uh . . . it scares me . . ." admitted Satish.

"Hmmm," mused Mr. Ramirez, "I'm not sure I can help you with that one. I was nervous every time I asked a new girl out, even into my late twenties."

"You're joking, right?" Satish asked, his eyes getting wide.

"Maybe," replied his coach, chuckling again. "But think of it as walking up to the free throw line with seconds left in a tie game. You start sweating. You think, will I make it and win or screw up and miss? Seems like the end of the world, but it isn't. Let's get back to practice. Maybe I'll have you start with a few free throws."

But think of it as walking up to the free throw line with seconds left in a tie game. You start sweating. You think, will I make it and win or screw up and miss?

## Think About It

- Do you get nervous when talking to someone you are interested in dating?

- Have you ever felt scared about asking someone out on a date?

- Do you know anyone who has admitted that he feels nervous or awkward about dating?

Everyone grows up at different rates. Maybe you've started to think about dating or kissing, but your best friend hasn't yet—or vice versa. In middle school and high school, adolescents of both sexes start becoming interested in each other in new ways. Teasing Satish was one way the girls were showing they were interested. Unfortunately, it made Satish uncomfortable because he wasn't ready for that kind of relationship.

A guy who's not ready to date when all his friends are might feel uncomfortable. But guys like Satish are normal. There is no set schedule for when a person should begin to date. Individuals vary widely in their development of romantic interests. There are guys who do not date until late adolescence. Some do not date until they are adults. And some cultures have different expectations about when a person should begin dating.

Maintaining good ties with your group of friends can often deflect some of the bullying and offer you support and understanding. In addition, it may help to find a trusted adult to talk to. He or she can help you work through your concerns and feelings and avoid doing something you may regret afterward.

## Work It Out

1. Respect yourself and your readiness, or lack of readiness, to date. There is no law that says one must date by a certain age.

2. If someone's taunting you about not wanting to date yet, talk to a trusted adult about it. You do not have to handle this situation alone.

3. Read up on the subject. By reading about dating, you can discover why people decide to start dating or choose to wait, and this will help you understand your own level of readiness.

## The Last Word from Pete

Group gatherings such as going to the mall are a good introduction to getting to know girls. It is times like these when you can develop good conversational skills and begin establishing a friendship that could later turn into a date. In the meantime, you can practice one-on-one interactions such as helping a classmate with schoolwork or lines for the school play. When should you start dating? That is different for everyone, but if you have been practicing your social skills you will find it much easier to talk to your date when you do start.

# 6

# Insecurity

Rejection hurts. Sometimes it is easy to tell why you were rejected. Sometimes you make an obvious mistake—getting so nervous you call a girl by the wrong name or something. Other times, you know what you were doing was wrong—asking out a friend's girlfriend, for example. Or perhaps outside circumstances, such as poor timing, made things just not work out right.

Often, however, it can be difficult to tell why that person said no. Maybe she gave you a reason, but it doesn't make sense. Maybe she didn't give any explanation, leaving you wondering what went wrong.

When faced with rejection, you might look for something or someone to blame. Some guys will blame themselves, thinking if they were cooler, smarter, or different in some way, it would have worked out. Other guys might blame the girl, thinking she must have been mean or stuck-up or she would have said yes. Aaron has trouble getting girls to go out with him, and he blames a number of different factors for it. His biggest problem, however, is his own insecurity.

*Often, however, it can be difficult to tell why that person said no.*

## Aaron's Story

Aaron was upset. He bought tickets to a show but none of the girls would go with him. "I have dance lessons that night," said Amanda, "But maybe . . . "

"Fine," snapped Aaron, cutting Amanda off midsentence. "Your loss. Hey Heather," he hollered, turning and walking toward the other girl. "This is your chance. I've got tickets to a show tomorrow night."

"I don't like their music," she told him.

"Whatever. Your loss!"

He asked several other girls, but each said she was busy. Aaron began to think they were lying.

"It's because I'm fat," he told himself, looking in the mirror the morning of the show. He sucked in his gut, then let it out again. "That's why girls won't go out with me."

## Think About It

- why do you think Aaron is having trouble finding someone to go to the show?

- If Aaron had allowed Amanda to finish her sentence, what do you suppose she might have said to him?

- Do you think Aaron's quick judgments and actions allow him to make many new friends?

Aaron ended up inviting his friend Joe at the last minute. Later, at the show, he saw Heather dancing in the aisle. She had told him she didn't like the band's music.

"Liar!" he hollered at her, knowing the music was too loud for her to hear him.

"What'd you say?" Joe inquired, giving him a quizzical look.

"Nothing," he replied, shaking his head but still looking down toward the dancing girl.

Joe followed his stare down the aisle. "Hey, there's Heather dancing in the aisle," he said, looking back at Aaron. "We should go say hi."

"I'm not talking to her. She lied to me."

"Heather?" asked Joe, astonished. "Why do you think Heather lied to you?"

Aaron just frowned at Joe and then went back to watching the group on the stage. On their way out after the show, Joe asked Aaron, "What happened between you and Heather?"

"Nothing," said Aaron. "She's just like all the girls around here, mean and stuck-up. They all think I'm fat. That's why I can't get a date."

"Heather called you fat?"

"No, but I know that's what she thinks. I asked her to this show and she said she didn't like the music. You saw her dancing. She lied to me because I'm fat."

He saw Heather dancing in the aisle. She had told him she didn't like the band's music.

"I doubt that."

"No one wants to date a fat guy," complained Aaron.

"I hate to be the one to tell you this," replied Joe, "but being fat isn't why you can't get dates."

## Think About It

- why do you think Aaron said that Heather thinks he is fat, even though she didn't say it?

- Do you believe that Aaron is cursed to never have dates because of his weight?

- If you were Aaron's friend, what advice might you give him about dating and talking to girls?

"Yeah it is," argued Aaron, "and it's not my fault. We eat out all the time."

"Then work out more, stupid," said Joe.

"Wouldn't work. It's genetic. My whole family is fat," Aaron assured him.

"Okay, so you're fat," agreed Joe, giving up on that line of argument. "So what? Look at Bai. He weighs a lot more than you, and he gets girls."

"He's got money so he can buy dates," said Aaron flatly.

"Bai's a nice guy. And super confident. He doesn't have to buy dates," Joe disagreed.

"Well, I'm a nice guy," Aaron insisted.

"Maybe you're nice," explained Joe, "but you're totally insecure."

"No, I just know what everyone's thinking," Aaron disagreed. "I don't know why I even bothered asking Heather out. I knew she'd say no."

"You don't give people a chance," Joe countered. "You're too busy assuming they're thinking bad things about you."

## Think About It

- Do you agree with Joe's assessment of Aaron?

- Do you feel that what Joe is saying to Aaron is helpful?

- Do you have any friends like Aaron? If so, how does their attitude affect your friendship?

Turning the corner while glaring at Joe, Aaron bumped into a girl who was standing there looking in a store window. "See what I mean? I take up the whole sidewalk."

"Excuse us," said Joe, looking at the stunned girl and shrugging his shoulders apologetically. Then turning quickly back to Aaron, he added, "You're exaggerating, man."

"You don't get it. You're too skinny," said Aaron. "Maybe you should try to understand what I have to put up with."

Joe and Aaron walked a few more blocks in silence before Joe turned to Aaron and snapped, "I'm getting sick of you and your attitude. And all the girls are, too!"

"Well, fine, then. Who needs you, anyway!" shouted Aaron. He gave Joe a shove and stomped off.

## Think About It

- why do you think Aaron is so focused on his weight?

- why did Aaron and Joe fight? what could each guy have done differently in this situation?

If a relationship doesn't turn out the way you had hoped, it can be difficult to figure out what went wrong. Sometimes, imagining that you are in the other person's shoes can help you figure things out.

In learning the skills of dating, the communication skills involved with conflict negotiation are important. Guys who blame everything that goes wrong on one real or imaginary problem, such as Aaron's assertion that everyone says he is fat, can have higher rates of social anxiety and depression. They are frequently lonelier than their peers, and they have lower self-esteem.

If you have a friend like this, you may be frustrated with trying to help him. You might be able to convince him to talk to a guidance counselor or adult mentor who can help him with self-esteem or anger management. You may find that your own frustrations in dealing with your friend become so great that you need to speak with a trusted adult yourself.

## Work It Out

1. Attitude is everything. If you are having difficulty getting dates, take a moment to

think of the types of people you like. Do you behave like someone you might date?

2. Talk to your friends and support persons about how they have asked someone out on a date and succeeded.

3. Read up on the subject of dating. There are tons of books and magazines with tips on how to ask girls out.

4. If someone turns you down for a date, it is okay for you to ask why. Sometimes, not knowing why you have been rejected is as bad as the rejection itself.

## The Last Word from Pete

Being rejected is difficult, but being difficult will get you rejected. If you have a negative attitude, you may find your rate of rejection is higher than other boys. Unless you learn to lighten up a bit, you may just have to live with yourself. But there are many reasons for rejection that have little to do with you. It could be a simple reason, like the girl is already dating someone else or she has a family event that night. If a girl declines an invitation, you could ask her why. If she tells you, you can learn from it. If she won't, be polite and don't push the conversation. Keep your cool, no matter what. Who knows, you just might want to date one of her friends in the future.

Brandon turned on the television and sat flipping channels. After a while his mom came in and asked him, "Where's Jamie? I thought you two were going to the mall tonight."

"He's busy!" was all he said in reply before turning the television off and heading for his room.

## Think About It

- Do you think Brandon is upset?

- Have you ever canceled plans with a friend so that you could go on a date?

- Do your friends visit you less frequently when they are dating someone?

The next day, Brandon sat around the house waiting to hear from his friend. "Where r u?" asked Brandon, leaving another unanswered text message on Jamie's phone.

"W/ amber call u l8r," Jamie finally texted back.

"L8r when?" Brandon typed, but there was no reply.

On Christmas Eve, Brandon had gone with his older sister Maddy to do some last-minute shopping at the mall. "Where is Jamie?" Maddy asked. "I haven't seen him since I got home from college."

think of the types of people you like. Do you behave like someone you might date?

2. Talk to your friends and support persons about how they have asked someone out on a date and succeeded.

3. Read up on the subject of dating. There are tons of books and magazines with tips on how to ask girls out.

4. If someone turns you down for a date, it is okay for you to ask why. Sometimes, not knowing why you have been rejected is as bad as the rejection itself.

## The Last Word from Pete

Being rejected is difficult, but being difficult will get you rejected. If you have a negative attitude, you may find your rate of rejection is higher than other boys. Unless you learn to lighten up a bit, you may just have to live with yourself. But there are many reasons for rejection that have little to do with you. It could be a simple reason, like the girl is already dating someone else or she has a family event that night. If a girl declines an invitation, you could ask her why. If she tells you, you can learn from it. If she won't, be polite and don't push the conversation. Keep your cool, no matter what. Who knows, you just might want to date one of her friends in the future.

# 7
# Feeling Forgotten

**E**ven if two guys have been close friends for years, a friendship can be tested when one of the friends finds a girlfriend and begins to focus all his attention on her. If this happens to you, you might feel as though your friend has suddenly abandoned you. You might also struggle with feelings of sadness, anger, and the loss of a friendship.

This experience can be one of the more bewildering adjustments a guy may make as he watches a close companion moving on without him. It is often a time of frustration for the guy left behind. All friendships that experience this disruption are altered in some way, and a few friendships do not survive it. But having a bit of patience, understanding, and good communication can help a friendship through this situation.

## Brandon's Story

Ever since second grade, Brandon and Jamie had been best friends. It was a rare day when they were

*Having a bit of patience, understanding, and good communication can help a friendship survive.*

not together. They loved baseball and spent hours playing catch. In Little League they were a great team, with Brandon at shortstop and Jamie at first base. They grew into the stars of the school team. Both guys were popular, easygoing, and ready to help others.

The last time Brandon saw his friend, Jamie was talking with Amber as school let out for Christmas break. "See you tonight," Brandon said, since they were planning to meet up at the mall.

"Later!" replied Jamie.

Brandon called Jamie's house after dinner and Jamie's mom answered, "Hi, Brandon, you just missed him. Jamie left about ten minutes ago."

Brandon sent a text message, "Where r u? c u 2night?"

A little later that evening, Brandon received a text message from Jamie saying he was at a movie with Amber.

Brandon turned on the television and sat flipping channels. After a while his mom came in and asked him, "Where's Jamie? I thought you two were going to the mall tonight."

"He's busy!" was all he said in reply before turning the television off and heading for his room.

## Think About It

- Do you think Brandon is upset?

- Have you ever canceled plans with a friend so that you could go on a date?

- Do your friends visit you less frequently when they are dating someone?

The next day, Brandon sat around the house waiting to hear from his friend. "Where r u?" asked Brandon, leaving another unanswered text message on Jamie's phone.

"W/ amber call u l8r," Jamie finally texted back.

"L8r when?" Brandon typed, but there was no reply.

On Christmas Eve, Brandon had gone with his older sister Maddy to do some last-minute shopping at the mall. "Where is Jamie?" Maddy asked. "I haven't seen him since I got home from college."

"Dunno. He disappeared when break started. He's hanging out with Amber all the time," said Brandon.

"Well, you'll see him tomorrow at Christmas dinner. He is still coming over, isn't he?" said Maddy.

"Probably not," mumbled Brandon.

When Brandon got home from shopping, his mom told him that Jamie had been by.

"where r u?" asked Brandon, leaving another unanswered text message on Jamie's phone.

"Jamie dropped off your Christmas gift," she said, adding, "He said he was sorry but he isn't able to come for dinner on Christmas. I told him you would be home soon and he could wait, but he said he had gotten a ride from a friend's mom and they were waiting outside. Did Jamie get a girlfriend?"

"That's what it sounds like," said Maddy.

"I don't know and I don't care," snapped Brandon as he headed for his room.

## Think About It

- Do you think Brandon really means it when he says, "I don't know and I don't care"?
- Do you think Jamie is handling the situation well?

In his room, Brandon turned on his computer. There was a Facebook message from Jamie. "Hope you like the present. Going to Amber's tomorrow. Call u l8r. Merry Xmas!"

"Whatever . . ." said Brandon, shoving his chair back from his desk as someone knocked on his bedroom door.

"Hey Brandon," called Maddy, "you left Jamie's present in the kitchen."

"I don't want it," he grumbled.

"Yes you do," said his sister, opening his door and coming into his room. "Jamie is your best friend and you need to remember that."

"Maybe he should've sent the present to his girlfriend."

"You're just feeling left out," replied Maddy.

"Well, I'm not that worried about that loser," he huffed.

"He hasn't dropped you as a friend," continued Maddy. "He's focused on a girl now, and it's inconvenient that it's happening over Christmas break."

"Yeah! Great timing."

"Maybe it isn't," smiled Maddy, "but think how bad it would be if he were this distracted during baseball season!"

Brandon's phone started to beep. It was a text from Jamie.

"Come over n play Madden?"

"See?" said Maddy. "You guys will be okay."

## Think About It

- If you were Jamie, what might you have done to let Brandon know that you were still friends?

- Can you think of two actions that Brandon could have taken in order to enjoy his Christmas break even though his best friend was so preoccupied?

- Have you ever found yourself being short with family members because you were upset with a friend?

When a friend becomes focused on a new girlfriend, we can feel a sense of loss that comes quickly and without warning. You may find yourself feeling hurt, abandoned, or betrayed. You may believe the friendship is over and feel sad because of that loss. You may become angry with your friend, but directing that anger at family or other friends won't help. Directing it at your friend or his new girlfriend won't help, either.

If this happens to you, try spending more time with some of your other friends. Some of them may have been in this situation before. Spending time with other friends allows you to get out and have fun rather than sitting at home alone brooding over your loss. Try to give your friend the space and time he needs to explore his new relationship.

## Work It Out

1. Though our dating relationships may come and go, our friends are there to help us get through all the time in between. Make sure to stay in touch with your friends and family while dating.

2. Talk to an adult. Adults have already experienced some of these same things.

Realize that what you are going through is a common experience.

3. If your best friend suddenly becomes very involved with someone they are dating, it is a great opportunity for you to get to know other friends better.

4. If your friend is feeling left out, a good way to assure him that you still consider him a close friend is to give him a call. It's okay to talk about your new relationship, but be sure to listen to what's going on in your friend's life, too.

## The Last Word from Pete

It's surprising how quickly even your best friend might seem to forget you when he becomes involved in a romantic relationship. Your friend's attention might be so focused on his new relationship that he might as well be a stranger. With time, your friendship may find a balance with the romance and continue more or less as it was.

Sometimes, however, the friendship ends. If that happens, it can be a difficult time. Hopefully you have a group of other friends to help you through the loss. Join a new club or sport and start getting to know new people.

# 8

# Moral Dilemma

uring adolescence, most of a guy's friends are typically the people he sees every day at school. Because of this, there is a good chance that the person a guy wishes to date has already dated someone he knows. This usually doesn't cause any problems. However, what if you become attracted to a girl who recently dated one of your close friends? You don't want to hurt your friend, but you do want to date the girl.

This can cause a moral dilemma. You don't want to be the jerk who betrays his friend or is insensitive to that friend's continued feelings for his ex. If you begin to date a girl soon after your friend has broken up with her, you could run the risk of being accused of stealing her. But even if he doesn't accuse you of anything, hard feelings can develop. Your friend might become jealous or angry, while you get defensive of your actions.

## Darius's Story

Darius met Tonya when his best friend Eric reluctantly introduced them. Though Darius had suspected for a

*what if you become attracted to a girl who recently dated one of your close friends?*

couple of weeks his friend was seeing someone, Eric had been keeping his girlfriend a secret. He might never have introduced them but for the fact that Darius had stopped by Eric's house when Tonya happened to be there.

"Hi," said Darius and Tonya in unison as a frowning Eric introduced them.

"I've never seen you around before," Darius continued.

"I go to Central," Tonya said smiling.

"You never said you were dating someone," Darius said to Eric. Darius was happy his friend had a girlfriend, but he was curious about why Eric hadn't said anything. "Where have you two been hiding?"

"It's none of your business," snapped Eric. "Can't you see we're busy here?" he grumbled, glaring at his friend.

"Yeah, I can see that," said Darius. "You don't have to bite my head off. I'll catch you later."

Turning back to Tonya, Darius added, "Maybe I'll see you around, too?"

"I hope so," smiled Tonya as he left.

A few days later, Darius and Tonya bumped into each other at the mall. "Hey, Tonya," Darius smiled. "What's up?"

"Nothing much," smiled Tonya. "Are you here with anyone?"

Still, he also wondered what Eric would think if he asked Tonya out. "You're sure it's over?"

"No, I'm just getting a new video game. You?"

"I was going to see a movie with my friend, but she ditched me. We already bought the tickets, though," Tonya explained in a rush. "Wanna come with me instead?"

"Great! But . . . you're going out with my friend."

"We broke up like the day after you stopped by," Tonya assured him. "It wasn't working out."

Darius had been attracted to Tonya from the start, so he was happy about the news. Still, he also wondered what Eric would think if he asked Tonya out. "You're sure it's over?"

"Yep, it's fine," she replied.

## Think About It

- Have you ever been interested in dating one of your friend's current or former girlfriends?

- Do you think it is okay to date one of your friend's ex-girlfriends? Why or why not? How long after the breakup should you wait?

- Do you think that it was okay for Darius to go to the movie with Tonya?

After the movie, Tonya and Darius started spending a lot of time together. There was no hiding their new relationship for long—Eric found out within a few days.

"You stole my girlfriend!" yelled Eric, crossing the street toward his friend.

"Did not!" said Darius. "She told me you weren't working out even before I met her."

"We were fine until you came along," Eric shot back at him.

"Come on, Eric," Darius replied. "You know it wasn't working. It wasn't my fault."

"Nice friend," sneered Eric sarcastically. He turned to walk away. "Thanks a lot."

"Eric!" he called to his friend's back. "Come back! I didn't do anything wrong. You can't be that mad at me." But Eric was gone.

Darius walked home slowly through the park, mulling over the fight.

*I didn't steal Eric's girlfriend,* he thought. *He doesn't have any reason to be mad at me. But would I have tried to steal Tonya if they hadn't broken up already?*

"Nice friend," sneered Eric sarcastically. He turned to walk away. "Thanks a lot."

Darius realized he didn't know the answer to that question. If he said yes, then Eric was right and he was a jerk. He didn't want to think of himself as a jerk. "I don't have to answer that question," he muttered out loud, breathing a sigh of relief. "They broke up before we started dating. Eric can't be mad at me."

## Think About It

- Do you feel that Darius stole Eric's girlfriend, or is Eric overreacting because he still has feelings for Tonya?

- Do you think that Darius should have asked Eric if it was okay to date Tonya?

- Do you think it is fair that Eric is angry at Darius?

Life is filled with conflicting feelings and dilemmas. Liking a friend's former girlfriend can be complicated. You don't want to hurt your friend, but you don't want to lose the girl, either. You may question your own motives. Did you behave honorably? If you get defensive in an argument, is it because you are in the right, or because you don't like the truth?

If your friend is open to talking, you might discuss how you both feel and come to an understanding. If that isn't possible, be patient and wait a little bit. A little time might work wonders. In the meantime, don't brag about dating the girl. Try seeing things from your friend's perspective.

If it is your ex-girlfriend, try to keep an open mind toward your friend. While it may be difficult, you'll need to learn to let go someday.

## Work It Out

1. If you are interested in dating a girl who has dated your friend, ask yourself what you would want your friend to do if the girl was your ex and take that course of action.

2. Ask permission if you value your friendship and know that the girl you are interested in has recently broken up with your best friend. Your friend may ask you not to date the girl yet, or he may admit that he doesn't mind if you do. One way or the other, your friend will know that you respect his feelings.

3. If your friend still has feelings for the girl and you feel it is too soon to date her, consider other options. Instead of starting with a romantic date, start by getting to know one another as friends. Maybe the right time will come later.

## The Last Word from Pete

You've broken up with your girlfriend, and the next thing you know, your best friend has asked her out. Is he a jerk? You didn't think so until this moment. So what has changed to make you angry with him? Is he insensitive to your feelings? Are you jealous? Or are you angry because you thought you could still work things out with your ex?

In time, you may realize your friend is innocent. If you are honest with yourself you may see that no one is really at fault. Sometimes we need to practice communicating with ourselves so we can communicate better with others.

# Breaking Up

**W**hen the person you have been dating suddenly ends the relationship, you have to deal with letting go. Sometimes the relationship was brief, and neither person had deep feelings for the other. Sometimes the breakup is mutual. But how do you deal if you weren't ready for the relationship to end?

Devon thinks the world is ending when his girlfriend Alexis dumps him unexpectedly. Getting over a breakup can be hard if you felt intense feelings for the other person. You might have felt as though the relationship would last forever. Filling that void in your life and finding other things to do with your time can be tough. One guy might react in anger, lashing out at the girl or at other people who care for him. Another guy might retreat into himself, hiding in his room or replaying the breakup over and over in his head. Neither of these are healthy reactions, but when you are in pain it is more difficult to make smart decisions.

## Devon's Story

Alexis was Devon's first girlfriend ever. They had been dating for a month. Alexis let Devon hold her hand in the halls at school. Last week, they had even kissed for the first time. Devon had feelings for Alexis that he'd never felt for anybody before. He thought it might be love.

*Getting over a breakup can be hard if you felt intense feelings for the other person.*

On Saturday morning, Devon got a text message from Alexis. "Can u come over? Need 2 talk."

"After lunch," he texted back.

When Devon reached Alexis's house she opened the door, looking solemn. "Hi, Devon, come in."

Devon's stomach sank. He could tell Alexis wasn't happy. They sat down on the couch in the family room.

"Devon," Alexis began. "Last weekend was weird."

"Uh, really?" stuttered Devon. "I thought it was really great."

"Listen, I started thinking about it. Kissing didn't feel right. I'm not ready for this."

"Well, okay," replied Devon. "We don't have to kiss anymore until you're ready."

Alexis shook her head. "No, I'm not ready to have a boyfriend at all. I want to break up."

"But Alexis—I think I love you!"

"I think you should leave."

"I'm sorry," he mumbled, more to himself than Alexis, as he walked out.

## Think About It

- Have you or a friend ever experienced a breakup? What happened? How did you handle it?

- Do you think Devon really loves Alexis?

Devon walked home after he left Alexis's house. "Now what do I do?" he kept repeating to himself. When he got home he sat in his room looking through comics. "Why?" he kept wondering aloud. Losing Alexis felt terrible. His stomach ached. He didn't understand what went wrong. Everything had felt great to him.

The comics didn't make him feel better. Feeling lonely and miserable, he wandered back downstairs.

"Hey Devon," said his youngest brother, Mike, as he ran through the kitchen. "You're back. Now we can play two-on-two." Without waiting to hear Devon's reply, he was out the door.

"Not interested," replied Devon, slumping glumly at the kitchen table.

"Not interested in what?" his mom said, coming into the room. "You're back early. Did your friend have something else happening today? I'm heading out," she continued. "We'll have dinner as soon as I get back from the store. Have you seen David?" Devon held his hands over his ears, blocking her voice as he wondered which of her questions to answer first.

"Mom," he started to say. "I have . . . " He stopped. He was on the verge of asking his mother for advice, when he saw she was out the back door and halfway to the car.

"I guess she doesn't care," he said, picking up his cell phone. He held it, playing with it for a few minutes before putting it down. Then he picked it up again, finally dialing Alexis's number.

"Alexis's phone, leave a message," the voice mail greeting said as he hung up.

"I guess she doesn't care either," he sighed.

## Think About It

- why do you think Devon feels that no one cares about him? Do you think it is true that no one cares?

- Have you ever wanted to talk to someone about something that was bothering you, but stayed quiet because the person seemed too busy to really listen to you?

"Hey Devon, you coming?" yelled his older brother Dave from the backyard.

"What do you want?" Devon said, heading outside.

In the driveway his brothers Dave and Mike were playing one-on-one as his other brother, Bill, watched.

"About time you got out here," Bill said. "I thought I'd have to forfeit this game."

"So what?" Devon grumbled. "My life is ruined."

"Right! Come on, drama queen, let's play," Bill said unsympathetically.

"What's the matter?" asked Mike.

"Alexis broke up with me," Devon replied, his voice cracking a little.

"Too bad," Mike responded, throwing a quick pass to Dave.

"That's not the end of the world," Dave said as he shot the ball. "Two points!"

Bill took the ball and waited a moment for Devon to be ready. "Wake up," he hollered, bouncing

the ball off Devon's shoulder. "Stop moping or we'll lose. Are you playing or pouting?"

Dave recovered the ball, throwing it quickly to Mike. "Four–zip," yelled Mike as he shot the ball through the basket from the left side.

"No competition," he snickered to Dave. "He's pouting," he said to Bill.

"I'm not pouting," Devon yelled back, missing another pass from Bill.

"Then pay attention to the game," grouched Bill. "I don't want these two bragging about how they skunked us."

"You just need to get over it," laughed Dave, sinking another basket. "But do it after this game is over."

"Get over it?" said Devon. "I thought we'd be together forever."

"Well, you thought wrong," Bill said, throwing another pass to Devon and rolling his eyes. "Quit being so dramatic and score some points."

"Score your own points," grouched Devon, throwing the ball into the yard and storming back to the house.

## Think About It

- What are Devon's brothers doing to try to make him feel better? Is it working? What else could they have done to help Devon?

- Do you think Devon should be able to just get over Alexis and move on?

Often when a relationship ends, only one of the people involved wanted it to be over. When someone breaks up with you, you may become sad, depressed, angry, or withdrawn. These emotions are normal, but they are also not healthy if they continue for a long period of time.

Breaking up leaves an emotional hole. It also leaves you with extra time on your hands, since you aren't seeing that person anymore. While spending some time alone is normal and will help you process your feelings, moping alone lets you dwell on your hurt feelings and will only make you feel bad for longer. It is important to let your circle of friends and family help you through these types of difficult times. They'll cheer you up, keep you away from negative behaviors, and help you find constructive things to do instead.

## Work It Out

1. After a breakup, take some time to be alone and process what has happened. But remember, too, to call upon your support group of friends and family.

2.  Try activities that help you relax. This might be anything from tough physical activity to listening to classical music—anything that helps you clear your head.

3.  Remember, breaking up is hard for everyone. The emotions you feel are natural and normal. But if you don't start to cheer up before long, you might consider speaking with a trusted adult or counselor.

## The Last Word from Pete

The ending of a first relationship can be the most difficult of all. You experience negative feelings unlike anything you've experienced before. You have to adapt socially to a lost relationship. And everything is new, so you have no prior experiences to guide your actions. Don't be afraid to speak up and ask a parent, older sibling, or other trusted adult for advice. Your experiences and feelings are not uncommon—nearly everyone goes through at least one breakup in his or her life. And everyone has to get over that person he or she lost.

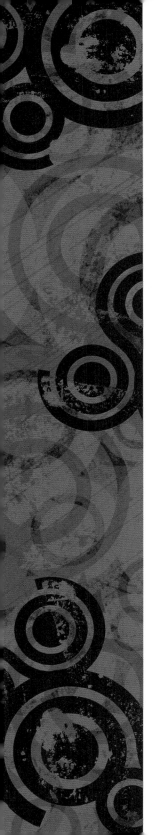

# 10
# Rumor Has It

uring adolescence, it can seem like keeping up your image is the most important thing of all. You might worry about how you look, whether you are liked, or what others think of you. Have you ever told a tale about someone that wasn't true just so you could feel bigger in front of the other guys?

Some guys might try to make themselves appear more important or more experienced so that others will look up to them. Watch out for exaggerated stories, especially if the guy seems to be making it up as he goes along. Paul has always looked up to Levi. Levi is a little older, and he likes to brag to the guys, especially the ones younger than he is. But these stories have a way of taking on a life of their own, growing and spreading with each new telling. We call them rumors. Rumors can seriously hurt others, creating false impressions and destroying reputations in the process.

## Paul's Story

Paul, Sam, and Alex were in the locker room at the rec center when Paul saw Levi heading their way. "Hey, Levi," said Paul. "What's up?"

"Hey, guys," said Levi. "Not much. But you should have seen me last night."

*watch out for exaggerated stories, especially if the guy seems to be making it up as he goes along.*

"Why? What were you doing?" asked Sam.

"Oh, if you only knew," smiled Levi wickedly.

"What's that mean?" asked Alex.

Snickering, Levi replied, "I was with LeAnn."

"What did you do?" said Paul sarcastically. "Bump into her?"

"Tell me more," interrupted Sam. "What were you and LeAnn doing?"

"We were at the mall, just holding hands . . . " Levi said, implying much more.

"Make out!" exclaimed Sam, high-fiving Alex.

"With LeAnn?" cut in Paul. "No way!"

"Shut up!" yelled Alex and Sam, giving Paul a nasty look.

"Jealous," Levi smirked, looking at Paul. "You've never been on a date. You wouldn't know what to do with a girl if she sat in your lap." Laughing, he continued, "She couldn't keep her hands off me."

"She was probably fighting you off," mumbled Paul as the other boys glared at him.

"After a while we went to a movie," Levi sighed, closing his eyes as if he could see the big screen. "We started making out in the theater, so I don't remember what show we saw."

"You're a liar," said Paul angrily.

"Who cares?" said Sam. "It makes a good story."

"Yeah, just shut up and let him talk," repeated Alex, "or get lost."

"I bet LeAnn cares," said Paul, walking away.
"I'm not listening to this crap."

## Think About It

- why do you think Levi is bragging to a group of his friends about making out with LeAnn?

- why do you think Paul is so upset by the way the guys were talking about LeAnn?

- Have you ever overheard a conversation in which the guys were bragging about how far they have gone with girls? How did you respond?

As Paul walked home, he thought about LeAnn and what Levi was saying. "I don't think LeAnn would do that," Paul said to himself. "But . . . I don't know. Maybe they were making out."

Paul considered the possibility, but rejected it. He wondered why Sam and Alex were encouraging Levi. He started to feel bad that he'd just walked away instead of trying to make Levi stop.

A few days later, Paul was at the food court in the mall. He waved at Alex, who was sitting with a few other guys he knew at a table. When his food came, he went over to join them just as Alex was getting up to go.

"Hey man," Alex greeted Paul. "Later."

"Hey guys, what's up?" Paul said, sitting down in Alex's chair.

"You missed hearing about LeAnn," said Matt.

"What about LeAnn?" asked Paul.

"She goes all the way," said Rob hopefully.

"No she doesn't," retorted Paul.

"Oh, what that girl will do," exclaimed Matt grinning.

"What who will do?" asked Tynan, walking up to the table.

"Alex was just here telling us how far LeAnn went with Levi the other night at the movie."

"LeAnn," said Matt. "Alex was just here telling us how far she went with Levi the other night at the movie."

"All the way to third base," chirped Rob.

"Who started that rumor?" asked Tynan.

"Levi was bragging the other day," said Paul.

"He's lying," said Tynan. "LeAnn told him to get lost the other night at the mall. I was there when she told him."

"Well, I still think LeAnn is easy," smirked Rob.

"Shut up, creep," Tynan glared at Rob. Leaning in close to Rob, Tynan continued, "How would you like it for me to mention that you wet the bed?"

"That's a lie!" shot Rob, standing up and shoving Tynan. Rob turned red as Matt started to laugh at him.

Tynan stood his ground. Coldly, he said, "Remember that when you start spreading rumors." Then, standing up and looking around the table, Tynan nodded at Paul. "Let's get out of here."

## Think About It

- Do you ever repeat rumors? How do you feel when you spread gossip?

- If a classmate of yours was spreading rumors about one of your friends, how would you respond?

- Do you think Tynan was right to threaten Rob with rumors about him?

Because they are insecure, need to be the center of attention, or desperately want to fit in, some guys may resort to making up stories or bragging about conquests. If a guy is a good enough storyteller, he may find many guys to listen to him. Unfortunately, innocent people may be hurt by his rumors.

You may find yourself in a dilemma if you belong to a group that encourages this type of activity. You can voice your opinion that you don't think what they're saying is right, but you may find that stance removes you from the group. Try to find friends who share your values instead.

In a respectful relationship, the details of how you romantically express yourself with the person you are dating are private. It can be okay to talk to close friends about some of your experiences in order to give or receive advice, and to make sure what you are doing is safe and healthy. However, bragging loudly to a group of people is a mark of insecurity.

## Work It Out

1. Keep the details of your relationships to yourself. Talking about private things with other people can hurt your date's feelings.

2. Go with your gut instinct. If you feel that the way other people are speaking about your friends or classmates is inappropriate, then it is inappropriate.

3. Support, high-five, thank, and applaud your friends when they confide to you that they made respectful choices while dating rather than selfish ones. The more you support your friends, the greater support you will gain in return.

## The Last Word from Pete

Rumors are never a form of good communication. Bragging about the big fish that got away doesn't usually harm anyone, but bragging about what you did with a girl can be mean and hurtful, whether it is true or not. If a rumor is passed around, things can be exaggerated in the retelling. What you say about others is serious, and you need to be respectful. At times you may hear others spreading rumors. You can take a stand. Let the person speaking know that while everyone likes a good story, these types of stories are not acceptable to you.

As you and your peers explore new relationships and the changing dynamics of those relationships, you will experience new friendships and new types of relationships. Along with these new friendships you may find yourself struggling with many unexpected events. You may not experience all of them personally, but you will probably know someone who does.

You may be bewildered by some changes you experience in yourself or see in your peers as you all grow physically, mentally, and emotionally. Some of those changes are very exciting, though at the time they are happening to you, they may feel scary. Some are just plain frustrating. It may seem to you that you are being left behind as your peers begin to date and you don't. Don't worry about it. You will catch up later.

Somewhere along the way you will feel rejected for some reason. It might be because a girl you like breaks up with you, or says no when you ask her out, or your best friend seems to forget you as he focuses all of his attention on his new girlfriend. You will struggle with moral dilemmas: Do I date my friend's former girlfriend, or do I get mad at my friend for dating my former girlfriend?

When is it okay to talk to others about what I have experienced with a girl, and when is it not? Is it okay to do something just because I think others are doing it? How do I feel about others who brag or exaggerate their own experiences?

It might be challenging at times, but do your best to keep yourself in check physically. Think before you act. You might not have the words to describe what you're thinking or feeling, but violence is not the answer.

You are absorbing vast amounts of information and experience throughout adolescence. Try to keep an open mind, and talk freely with your peers, mentors, siblings, or parents about your questions, feelings, and frustrations. Improving your communication skills will help you get a leg up on the challenges you face.

Best of luck,
Pete

Remember, a healthful life is about balance. Now that you know how to walk that path, pay it forward to a friend or even yourself! Remember the Work It Out tips throughout this book, and then take these steps to get healthy and get going.

- Just because you start making out with someone does not mean that you have to continue doing it, especially if you suddenly begin to feel you are making a mistake.

- Don't worry if you begin to doubt or wonder about your own sexuality. This process is normal and healthy.

- Sometimes it can be difficult to judge the line between friend and girlfriend. Often, telling her your feelings will help you work things out.

- Each guy gets ready to date at his own pace. If you find that the guys around you are teasing you because you are not yet ready to date, find a trustworthy adult to talk to.

- When you ask a girl on a date, be confident and be yourself. You don't need to wear a special outfit, change your hairstyle, or buy anything.

- Instead of closing out the rest of the world, introduce your sweetheart to your friends. Arrange group get-togethers and stay connected.

- If you want to date a friend's ex, talk to him and see how he feels before you make a move. If a friend asks about your ex, answer honestly.

- If you experience deep heartache because of a breakup, call your friends and loved ones to come be with you. They can listen and help you pick up the pieces.

- If you are busy bragging to others about what you have experienced with particular girls, you are not only potentially damaging the girls' reputations, but also damaging your own reputation as a trustworthy guy.

- Always honor your girlfriends by keeping the details of how you express your love with one another between you and your girlfriend. Ask her permission first if you wish to share something with friends to make sure she is comfortable with it. Discuss things privately rather than publicly.

# Additional Resources

## Selected Bibliography

Collins, W. Andrew, and Brett Laursen. "Changing Relationships, Changing Youth: Interpersonal Contexts of Adolescent Development." *The Journal of Early Adolescence* 24 (2004): 55–62.

Hand, Laura Shaffer, and Wyndol Furman. "Rewards and Costs in Adolescent Other-sex Friendships: Comparisons to Same-sex Friendships and Romantic Relationships." *Social Development* 18 (May 2009): 270–287.

Miller, Shari, et al. "Early Adolescent Romantic Partner Status, Peer Standing, and Problem Behaviors." *The Journal of Early Adolescence* 29 (2009): 839–861.

## Further Reading

Gitchel, Sam, and Lorri Foster. *Let's Talk About S-E-X: A Guide for Kids 9–12 and Their Parents.* 2nd ed. Minnetonka, MN: Book Peddlers, 2005.

Madaras, Lynda, and Area Madaras. *My Body, My Self: For Boys.* New York: Newmarket, 2007.

Madaras, Lynda, and Area Madaras. *The "What's Happening to My Body?" Book for Boys.* New York: Newmarket, 2007.

Pfeifer, Kate Gruenwald. *Boy's Guide to Becoming a Teen: Getting Used to Life in Your Changing Body.* Ed. Amy B. Middleman. San Francisco, CA: Jossey-Bass, 2006.

# Web Sites

To learn more about understanding relationships and dating, visit ABDO Publishing Company online at **www.abdopublishing.com**. Web sites about understanding relationships and dating are featured on our Book Links page. These links are routinely monitored and updated to provide the most current information available.

# For more information:

For more information on this subject, contact or visit the following organizations:

**Gay, Lesbian, Bisexual, and Transgender National Help Center Hot Line**
1-800-246-PRIDE (Youth hotline)
www.GLBTnationalhelpcenter.org
This Web site has phone numbers and links to local organizations nationwide. It also features live online chats with counselors.

**The National Campaign to Prevent Teen and Unplanned Pregnancy**
1776 Massachusetts Avenue, NW, Suite 200
Washington DC 20036
202-478-8500
www.thenationalcampaign.org; www.stayteen.org
This group publishes information for teenagers about pregnancy, sex, love, and relationships.

# Glossary

### adolescence
The period from puberty to maturity.

### dilemma
A situation involving an unpleasant choice, a predicament.

### gay
Homosexual.

### heterosexual
A person who is sexually attracted to members of the opposite sex.

### homosexual
A person who is sexually attracted to members of the same sex.

### inadequate
Not enough.

### reputation

How one is generally regarded by others.

### sexual identity

How a person defines his or her sexual attraction for other people; can include homosexual, heterosexual, and other categories.

### straight

Heterosexual.

# Index

adults, 20, 26, 45, 54–55, 64, 74, 93
anxiety, 26, 44, 64. *See also* nervousness
apologies, 14–19, 32, 69, 72, 86
asking someone out, 36–45
attitude, 56–65
attraction, 20–27, 28–35

breaking up, 79–83, 84–93

communication, 11, 19, 34–35, 64, 67, 83, 101
conflict, 56–65, 79–83
confusion, 10, 19, 20–27, 30–35

dance, 36–43
dating
    going on a date, 40–43, 78–79
    readiness, 46–55
depression, 64, 92

embarrassment, 10–19, 36, 44–45, 99

fighting, 62, 99
friends
    attracted to, 25–27, 28–35
    former girlfriend, 76–83
    groups, 11, 14, 38, 43–44, 49, 54–55, 75, 93,
        94–101
    ignored by, 66–75
    kissing, 10–19

heterosexual, 20, 26–27
homosexual, 20, 22, 25, 26–27, 49–50

kissing, 10–19, 25, 27, 54, 85–86

making out. *See* kissing

nervousness, 19, 36–45, 52–55, 56. *See also* anxiety

parents, 23, 29–30, 41–43, 44–45, 67–68, 87–88, 93
peer pressure, 10–19, 21–22, 46–55
permission, 19, 76–83

rejection, 56–65, 66–75
reputation, 94–101
respect, 18, 51, 55, 83, 86, 94–101
rumors, 21–22, 94–101

sex, 21–27
shyness, 36–45, 46–55
siblings, 23, 68–72, 87–91

teasing, 46–55
trust, 24–25

## About the Author

Pete Heiden worked as a landscape architect specializing in natural resource and recreation projects throughout the West before returning to school and earning his MFA in writing. He is a poet and nonfiction writer who currently lives in Minnesota.

## Photo Credits

Yuri Arcurs/Shutterstock Images, cover, 3; Fotolia, 12, 15, 69; Chris Schmidt/iStockphoto, 16, 50; Slobo Mitic/iStockphoto, 22; iStockphoto, 24, 59; Shutterstock Images, 31; Vladimir Wrangel/Fotolia, 32; Daniel Schoenen/iStockphoto, 37; Christopher Pattberg/iStockphoto, 40; Tim Souza/iStockphoto, 42; Matty Symons/Shutterstock Images, 49; Christopher Phares/Shutterstock Images, 52; Stuart Monk/iStockphoto, 62; Horst Schmidt/Fotolia, 71; Willie B. Thomas/iStockphoto, 73; Jim DeLillo/iStockphoto, 78; Fernando Jose Vasconcelos Soares/Shutterstock Images, 80; Jason Stitt/Fotolia, 86; Duncan Walker/iStockphoto, 89; Theodore Scott/iStockphoto, 90; Bernardo Grijalva/Shutterstock Images, 96; Catherine Lane/iStockphoto, 98